AF354621

Musings Without The Muse

Poetry pilots from the master of none

Cibi Thomas

Copyright © Cibi Thomas
All Rights Reserved.

This book has been self-published with all reasonable efforts taken to make the material error-free by the author. No part of this book shall be used, reproduced in any manner whatsoever without written permission from the author, except in the case of brief quotations embodied in critical articles and reviews.

The Author of this book is solely responsible and liable for its content including but not limited to the views, representations, descriptions, statements, information, opinions, and references ["Content"]. The Content of this book shall not constitute or be construed or deemed to reflect the opinion or expression of the Publisher or Editor. Neither the Publisher nor Editor endorse or approve the Content of this book or guarantee the reliability, accuracy, or completeness of the Content published herein and do not make any representations or warranties of any kind, express or implied, including but not limited to the implied warranties of merchantability, fitness for a particular purpose.

The Publisher and Editor shall not be liable whatsoever...

Made with ❤ on the BookLeaf Publishing Platform
www.bookleafpub.in
www.bookleafpub.com

Dedication

I like to dedicate this book Sum1 who believes in me and makes me look better always. That Sum1 is Sumi, my better half.

Preface

What's the most common thing among people? Are they curious or are they having fear? I was surprised when Rae, my son, asked me this question. This is out of nowhere and nothing I can relate to, on how he might have got these words. All the more, when I myself was wondering on these words for some time. I had been thinking how "fear" crowds a lot of our emotions and therefore without a blink of an eye, perhaps that I could not control it, I replied it's fear and people are more fearful than curious. His innocent question might have been misplaced, but for him, curiosity was related to enthusiasm and fear related to boredom. True, ain't it? We fear for our family, our loved ones and the state of relationships because we fully are involved in them and we don't want any change in it other than an advancement. Does it mean love invokes fear? True love should drive away fear. Attachments? , is that the culprit? So what's the opposite of fear? What drives it away? Curiosity in Rae's world may mean adventure and willingness. Guess, that is one aspect of fear going off. Be curious and let it carry you over the tides of fear.
This book is a sum of curiosity overcoming fear, in poem, and its various forms.

Acknowledgements

Thank you to the metro, the iPhone and the notes that I felt like writing sometimes, sitting idle to commute. Thank you for the 11 PM winding up time and for the 11:30 PM friends on WhatsApp whom I could share with. Who would joke on it and say it is not understandable. It was then proved, that this is quite original to try for a publishing project. Thank you Bookleaf and the support team for patiently working on the newbie.

1. Haiku on festival of lights

Festive cheers for the lights outside
Groping in the world with darkness besides
Light of the heavens, unseen inside

2. Musings without the muse

Me. An artist with you.
Dull without you
I had a gift
I lost
I .....
No....
Not anymore
Not me, the old me
Now a lot more to go
Now the account opens
Now the new start of what I can be
Now to get to what I could be, want to be

3. Limericks-Sweat is real

It was fun, it was a laughter peal
Hard labor, toiled the tide for sweat to reveal
Hence proved right, was work's sweet appeal
Sweat is real -check the feel

4. Villanelle on Sports

It is time for your game, your fight, your story
For an hour of play, not years of talk, solves the query
In spirit, in skill, in mind , lies true glory

Old demons may slur, making you weary,
Shout out, hear nothing, abandon the fright, the worry,
It is time for your game, your fight, your story

Children with frail shots turning fiery,
Little men, yet big giants in a future diary
In spirit, in skill, in mind, lies true glory

Losing with a fight, is pride, not to be sorry,
Let strangers know your play, the heart's quarry
It is time for your game, your fight, your story

Those who worked on you, both bright and dreary
An equal act together, that shines on you pearly
It is time for your game, your fight, your story

That hour on your stage, play your song, while you stay
Bring on the court, your poem, your say
It is time for your game, your fight, your story
In spirit, in skill, in mind , lies true glory

5. Transit

I was caught in a stranded transit
Not planned, neither unexpected
A trip worth but not needed
So I think for the time so wasted

Or is it that indeed it was wasted?
In all your travel, haven't you tasted?
Not just the sweets, food and bread
But bored faces often restrained

Or is it true that time was badly spent ?
The WFH is a puzzled feeling to vent
A day and two sleepless nights
Red eye flights, artificial lights

Faces, shapes, colour and smells
Varieties that man of the world dwells
There must be a place between start and end
There might be a story from here to append

6. Friends

My friends are my missing parts
They hold my yearnings
Branches in trees
They grow with different learnings
Yet the tree stands beautiful
Extending unique leanings

7. The 5 AM Club

The 5 AM club
Is not a gathering of people
Is but some people broken
Some lonesome souls
With burns and bruises
Hurt in the heart before
I am one of them
Trace my 5 to some 3's
Waking up and not able to sleep
Remorse and recourse appearing steep
And once it was that action was done
To turn sleeplessness into an act of run
Punishing the heart for its vocal sin
Stretch it and pull it to make it outrun

8. Christ at the well

The well, that Jacob built
Waiting near the water
Thirst to quench
Hunger to do the Father's will
Christ, you are the light
Lighten our load
Load of our being
Being among the living
Burden of the past
A past that cringes
A cringe of conscience
A fall so cognizant
And here, you read me, see me
Said the woman at the well
Told me everything I have done
Your call to me, a heavy laden, now unburdened
You declared, the great " I AM "
Accepted me, as I am
Not the same world any more
Messiah, I run, I shout, ever and ever more

9. The perils of being born

Baby, they call you
And lo, you are on-board
A journey not your choice
The perils of being born

The elders started the same way
Not yet knowing the end stay
Alone in the world you are set apart
Don't you cry, you are just a start

Row, row, row your boat
Let the heart keep on the beat
Fellow men may leave their seat
Some new to come in and fit

10. Why write ?

Let me write
On what is left
To know what is right

Thoughts like a river,
Flows and immerses like pearls,
Some truths buried in their depths

Dive then, but don't pick up
For they live there
Meant there, and remain unseen

I had burnt my pages
Of poetry and proses
Reflecting my blushes

And when the fire consumed
Saw my words dying
And Innocence crying

Cursed me, I know they did
For those words are never again formed
Those thoughts, are still caged within

11. An absence of a presence

There are tears hidden in the air
Clouds with darkness suspended
A dusky time that foretells gloom
Something that is about to end soon

A pinch inside my heart I felt
Like a hole was just plugged
That route of an emotion escape
What has left me just now?

12. Trinity

Three to complete
Three truths that has been always
Triune, the union of three

The bread, the life and the truth
The soul, the nature and God
The father, the son and the holy spirit

13. Srikanth

If you my friend, were an angel of God

Would I have ever known?
A higher energy and an ever presence
Besides me and talking to me
Laughing about and yet concerned
Would I have know that you are part of God?
Who walks with me and eats with me
Same roof and our one big sky

And one day, he will have a reason to part
A shift of place, or a bond to attach
And then I will just be a person who knew
A Facebook friend or just a time he lived in the past

All the while his silence would shout
That he lived in the world without
An excuse for the exit
A cancer it was, be told
That limited time were pure gold

14. A cup of Tea

Art or science for the maker of the tea
A proportion to mix in liquid and fire
Water, milk and the powder down
Turning colours of white to brown

That he readies a special cuppa
An essence of time and taste
An idea distinct is his magic
And his work is such a play

Work is therefore to share
Your gifts and your fare
To bring in your magic and art
For the artist remains a king at heart

Your work is a cup of tea
A gift of flavour you put in,
That each day of work you log out
Completes a work of art,
Your signature, your style,
Your touch of heart

15. Parents

Our only true God on earth
Our parents who show us the strength
This chords of which we are made
Reach the potential, our duty laid

That which you hear often now
The Papa preach and the Mamma speak
Ignored often as a routine talk
With brothers , you remember it , later on

That which you eat hurriedly,
Regulation breakfasts and family meal
Reminiscing over an important deal
Real deal was the meal, will later reveal

Mother's stories are deep connections
A weave of nostalgic and detailed yarn
Those memoirs will be worn on me
On winter blues, to keep my warm

16. If I start today

If I start today,
to look inside and correct my wrongs,
I may start with you my dear
and ask you not to remember my moles

They are many to count,
And though you say, don't regret
My choices have not been great
Tell me you would forget

If I start today
to make myself grow
I would breathe in your bliss
And do it every day

You are my peace
And you have no idea
How I yearn it so
When I miss you the most

If I start today
To chase my dreams
I will write it on the wall
What I would think it to be

To refine my thoughts
And seek courage to do
To climb the sacred hill
That we call our makers' will

17. Runners

Sweating and running, my love, my life,
With each mile, how I feel alive,
The joy of endurance, the thrill of the chase,
Fuels my heart, and sets my pace.
In the company of friends, we share the road,
Together we strive, we push, we goad,
And when the race is run, our hearts full of glee,
We'll keep on running, for the love of being free.

18. Gaming

Of human bondage
In the machine learning age
Bots knowing more than men
Wisdom lynched by grown ups
Yet, so safe, she is with the children

The man's child plays games on I-pads inside
To the next level than yesterday
"Life" saved is all he wants

But for me, life is happening
When he is lost
In the moment
And in the greens outside

19. An unconventional living

Living conventional
Trusted ways
Followed path
Not easy, neither a big task

If life was so convenient,
Why would you be born?
Made by God to mend his garden

A vineyard worker you are
Wonderfully and fearfully made

So make some wine
Fire up your nerve
Dance in your vein
Ignite a mind

Give convenience a run
Do everything before undone
Make your passion the new norm
And normal wont be boring

20. Far Away

Our souls in the night have lived their years
Long lost souls that caught up on time

Seldom we met, but always by my bay
Even an OK would make my day

Distances- Ether or matter keep growing
Moments- Those frozen keep melting

Once a connection of signs
A noble moon , a secret manifest

Unread the other signs
of the waning moon, the distance between

How many times to lose you dear?
How many beliefs to kill if I may ?

Now the last one to go again
That
There is no such thing as far away

21. Alongside

I can walk you to home
No need you say
That's ok , for I can walk
Anyone can walk anywhere
It is allowed
So I can walk too
And anyone can jump
So I will jump in between
When I walk

But I will walk alongside
For anyone is allowed to walk anywhere

www.ingramcontent.com/pod-product-compliance
Lightning Source LLC
LaVergne TN
LVHW021719210726

843509LV00021B/2782